The 15 Greatest BOARD GAMES in the World

by the editors of **KLUTZ.**

What You Get

More than 15 games — carefully chosen for players of a variety of ages and talents

15 beautiful game boards

2 dice

44 reversible playing pieces

With one side up, you have
22 red pieces and
22 white pieces.

Flip 'em over and you have
11 blue, 11 yellow, 11 purple,
and 11 green pieces.

20 klutzner coins

16 tokens

for playing China Moon and Corsaro

12 pentominoes

shapes that offer intriguing mental challenges in Pentominoes

A storage drawer for your playing pieces

Open both ends of the box and slide the tray out. As you play use the tray to store the pieces you aren't using.

Open both ends — slide the tray out.

Push the box against the cover.

Store your pieces in the tray.

The box lies flat under the book while you play.

What You Need

A playful spirit, a willingness to think, and five real pennies for playing Push Penny Bounce. (Check under the sofa cushions.)

Who Plays First?

That's the first question people ask when they sit down to play a game. Here are some ways to choose the first player:

 Roll the dice.

 Let the next person with a birthday go first.

 Let the youngest person, or the best-looking person, or the person with the worst shirt go first.

The Pie Rule

Once you know who plays first, use the Klutz-certified Pie Rule to make sure that both players have an even chance of winning a two-player game.

When applied to splitting a piece of pie, this rule says: You cut the pie and I choose which piece I want.

When applied to board games, this rule says: You make the first move and I choose to claim that move as my own or make my own move.

Why these games?

When choosing games for this book, we followed a few simple rules.

The games are easy to learn. Read the instructions and you'll be playing in minutes.

You can play the games over and over, always discovering something new. These games all encourage players to plan ahead and think strategically.

The games appeal to a wide variety of players — of different ages, different talents, different attention spans. In many games, we include suggestions on how to give the underdog a fighting chance.

While creating our list of games, we consulted games experts R. Wayne Schmittberger who edits *Games Magazine* and Mark Jackson who specializes in playing board games. Then we consulted the real experts: kids at El Carmelo Elementary who cheerfully sacrificed their free time to play games with us.

After much playing and talking and testing, we ended up with the 15 best games in the world. Then we made them even better by shortening playing times, simplifying rules, and adding hints and tips to speed you to becoming an expert player. We gathered new ways to play familiar games and odd facts that you don't really need to know (but probably want to).

While creating this book, we had a great time. Now it's your turn.

Play fair. Have fun.

4

List of Games

6 hoppers
and Mini Hoppers
Close cousins of Chinese Checkers

Players: Two or four **Ages:** 7 and up
Playing time: 30–45 minutes

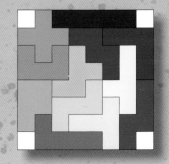

8 Game of Y
An easy game to learn with a lot of tricky strategy

Players: Two **Ages:** 8 and up
Playing time: 10 minutes

10 The Royal Game of Ur
Popular in ancient Sumeria and still fun today

Players: Two **Ages:** 7 and up
Playing time: 30–45 minutes

12 Surround
A game of "surround and capture" based on the ancient game of Go

Players: Two **Ages:** 8 and up
Playing time: 5–10 minutes

14 Corsaro

Escape Pirate Island with the help of the other players

Players: Two to four **Ages:** 8 and up
Playing time: 30 minutes

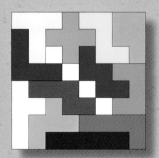

hoppers

In this game, your pieces hop across the board, jumping over other pieces.

Players
2 or 4

Ages
7 and up

Playing Time
30–45 minutes

You Need
10 playing pieces of the same color for each player

Setup
Each player takes his or her ten playing pieces and puts them on the colored squares in one corner of the board. If two people are playing, use two corners that are diagonally across from each other (the blue and the red corners, for example). If four people are playing, use all four corners.

Your Goal
Move your pieces from your corner into the corner diagonally across the board. Blue and red switch places, and so do yellow and purple.

Playing

Choose a player to go first. Players take turns, moving around the table. When it's your turn, you can step or hop.

To step, move one of your pieces one square in any direction, including diagonally.

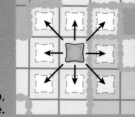

You can step, moving one space.

To hop, jump one of your pieces over another piece — either yours or your opponent's. The piece you hop over must be on a square right next to the square your piece is on, and you must land on an empty square. The piece you hop over is NOT removed from the board.

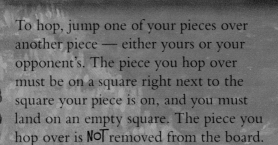

◀ **You can hop by jumping a piece.**

Or you can make ▶ multiple hops.

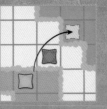

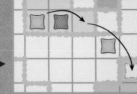

If the piece that has just hopped can make another hop (in any direction), you can hop again — or you can choose not to hop.

Winning

You win by being the first to move all your pieces from your corner into the corner diagonally across from yours.

A Special Rule

Some people (we're not naming names, but you know who you are) might leave a piece in their corner to prevent their opponent from fully occupying that territory. Or someone might hop into your target area to keep your pieces out. We have a rule just for these people: A corner is fully occupied if all the spaces are full — no matter what color the pieces are.

Hints and Tips

Try to set up a bridge — a line of pieces that lets a series of hops carry one of your pieces to the other side of the board. But watch out! Your opponent can use that same bridge.

Leveling the Field

If one player is much stronger than the other, let the weaker player go first and take an extra turn right at the beginning.

A Bonus Game

If you only have a few minutes, try playing Mini Hoppers using the 16-square area in the center of the board. Each player has six playing pieces. You win by moving all your pieces into the opposite corner, just as you do in Hoppers. But you can't move backward; only forward. Because the board is small, this is a very crowded game.

Starting board for Mini Hoppers

Game of Y

This is a very simple game to learn — and a tough one to master.

Players
2

Ages
8 and up

Playing Time
10 minutes

You Need
15 red playing pieces
15 white playing pieces

Your Goal
Connect all three sides of the game board with an unbroken chain of playing pieces.

Leveling the Field

If you are just a little better at this game than your opponent, let the other player go first to give him a small advantage. If the underdog needs more help, let him take an extra turn up front.

Stuff You Don't Need to Know

Physicist Craige Schensted and mathematician Charles Titus invented this game. Our game board has 30 spaces. For a challenge, play Y on a bigger board, like the board made by Kadon Enterprises, which has 89 spaces.

Playing

Players take turns placing one piece of their color on any unoccupied space on the board.

Each corner counts as belonging to the **TWO** sides of the board that it touches. You can connect all three sides by connecting a corner to the opposite side.

Winning

You win by connecting all three sides of the board with an unbroken chain of your playing pieces. Your chain of pieces can wander all over the board as long as it connects all three sides.

Hints and Tips

Think about how to place your pieces so that your opponent can't stop you from connecting them.

If white puts a piece on A, red can connect her pieces by putting a piece on B. If white puts a piece on C, red can connect to the side by putting a piece on D.

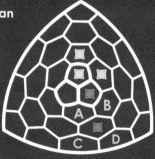

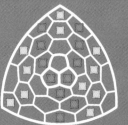

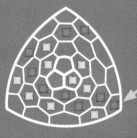

Here are two completed games. Red won both.

This corner piece connects two sides.

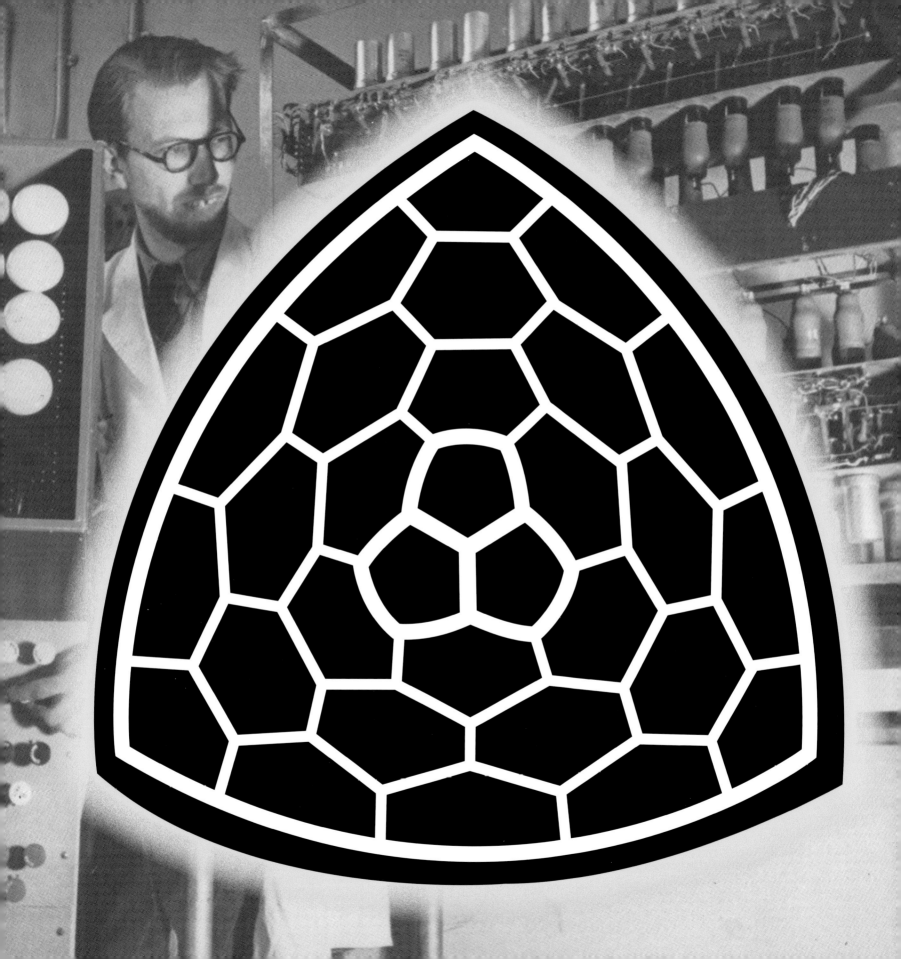

THE ROYAL GAME OF UR

Some 4,500 years ago in the Sumerian city of Ur, rich folks played a game like this one.

PLAYING

Players take turns. When it's your turn, flip the four coins and count the heads.

Move one of your five pieces that many spaces forward. You can move any piece, but only one piece.

Move forward, never backward. If you get all tails, you don't move at all. Better luck next time.

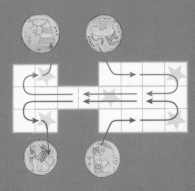

The red arrows show one player's path. The blue arrows show the other player's path. The paths overlap in the center of the board.

If your piece lands on a star, you get another turn. Good for you.

Only one piece can be on a space at a time. If you land on a space that your opponent is already on, you bump her piece back to her start. Too bad for her.

A piece on a star can't be bumped. And you can't bump your own piece. If a move would land you on an occupied star or on a space you're already on, choose a different move. If there aren't any other moves, you have to skip your turn.

To reach the finish, you must roll the exact number needed to leave the board.

WINNING

You win by being the first to reach the finish with all five of your pieces.

LEVELING THE FIELD

Give the underdog a better chance by letting him have a few do-overs. That is, if the underdog doesn't like the results of his coin flipping, he can flip all four coins again. Before you start playing, agree on how many do-overs the underdog gets. Decide whether the player must accept the result of the second try even if it's worse than the previous try.

FINISH

START

FINISH

START

STUFF YOU DON'T NEED TO KNOW

Archeologists found the rules for this game written on clay tablets in cuneiform, one of the earliest forms of writing.

SURROUND

Think of this as a game of cops and robbers — where the cops try to surround the robbers and the robbers try to surround the cops.

WANTED

PLAYERS 2

AGES 8 and up

PLAYING TIME 5–10 minutes

YOU NEED
22 red playing pieces
22 white playing pieces

YOUR GOAL
Surround one of your opponent's pieces.

PLAYING

When it's your turn, place one of your playing pieces on a manhole cover. Once you place a piece, you can't move it.

To surround an opponent's piece, you must put one of your pieces on every manhole cover directly connected to your opponent's piece.

This red piece has been surrounded by white pieces…

…so has this one.

You can also surround a group of pieces. Pieces of the same color make a group when streets directly connect them. Two pieces that are diagonally across from each other are not connected since no street runs directly from one to the other.

These three red pieces are a group.

This piece is not part of the group.

Pieces in a group can't be surrounded individually, but you can capture the whole group by surrounding it completely.

This group of red pieces has been surrounded.

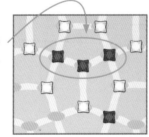

WINNING

Surround one of your opponent's pieces or a group of his pieces and you win the game.

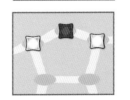

AN IMPORTANT FINE POINT

Placing a piece on a manhole cover that is already surrounded would be silly — unless that move lets you surround one of your opponent's pieces. If that move surrounds your opponent, then you win.

LEVELING THE FIELD

If you are playing a weaker opponent, let the underdog play first — and give him an extra turn at the beginning of the game.

HINTS AND TIPS

Some manhole covers on the edge of the board are connected to only two other manhole covers. This makes them easier to surround than others. As you play, pay attention to how many manhole covers are connected to the spot where you're putting your piece.

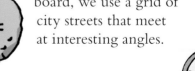

STUFF YOU DON'T NEED TO KNOW

This game is based on Go, a game of "surround and capture" that became popular in China over 3,000 years ago. Rather than a traditional Go board, we use a grid of city streets that meet at interesting angles.

Corsaro

Avast, matey! This is a cooperative game in which everyone tries to beat the pirates. All the players win together — or you all lose to the pirates.

Players 2 to 4

Ages 8 and up

Playing Time 30 minutes

You Need

12 playing pieces: 3 in each of 4 different colors
3 skull-and-crossbones tokens
2 dice
5 klutzner coins per player

Setup

Put a skull-and-crossbones token on each space marked with a skull and crossbones.

Put the playing pieces by the "Start" flag on the island in the middle of the board.

Give each player five klutzners.

Your Goal

Help everyone reach safety in the harbor of Santaijana.

Y

ou and the other players were shipwrecked on a desert island. You must work together to move your boats through pirate-infested seas to the safe harbor of Santaijana.

Playing

The playing pieces are boats. The skull-and-crossbones tokens are pirate ships.

With FOUR players, each player controls three boats of one color. With THREE players, anyone can move the boats of the fourth color. With TWO players, each player has six boats, three of one color and three of another.

Choose a player to go first, then move around the table, taking turns. On each turn, roll both dice. One die tells you how many spaces to move a boat. The other die tells you how many spaces to move a pirate ship. You choose which boat to move, which die to use for the boat, which die to use for the pirate ship, and which to move first — the boat or the pirate ship.

Boats leave the island on the blue spaces. Both boats and pirate ships move counter-clockwise on the yellow spaces. Several boats can be on the same space at the same time.

Pirates must stay on the yellow spaces, but boats can also use the safe passages marked by pink spaces. Each time you travel on one of these safe routes, you must place a klutzner on Pirate Island.

Capturing and Rescuing

Pirates capture a boat when a pirate ship passes or lands on the boat or when the boat passes or lands on a pirate ship. Captured boats go to Pirate Island. A pirate can capture more than one boat in a turn.

This pirate ship captures two boats because it passes one and lands on one.

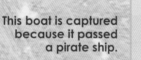
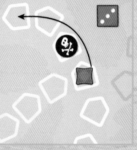

This boat is captured because it passed a pirate ship.

DON'T FORGET — you're working with the other players. You don't want to send them to Pirate Island. In fact, you want to help them escape the pirates.

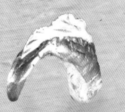

To rescue a captured boat, you must land a boat on a space marked with a life preserver. You or the boat's owner must pay the pirates one klutzner, putting the coin on Pirate Island. Without a coin, you can't free a boat. Put the rescued boat on the same space as the boat that rescued it.

A Few More Rules

If you have boats that can move, you have to move. (Boats on Pirate Island or in Santaijana harbor can't move.) If none of your boats can move, you must move someone else's boat. You must move a boat — even if it means capture by pirates.

Boats can pass each other. When you pass or land on the same space as another player's boat, you may give him a klutzner or take a klutzner from him.

Pirate ships can't pass other pirate ships. Only one pirate ship can be on a space.

You can move onto the green spaces that mark the safe harbor of Santaijana only if you roll the exact number needed. If you don't roll the number you need, stay put — or circle the pirate seas again.

Winning

The game ends when all boats are either captured or in Santaijana harbor. With four players, everyone wins if ten boats reach the harbor. With two or three players, everyone wins if 11 boats reach the harbor.

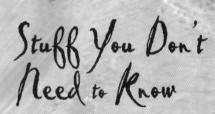

Stuff You Don't Need to Know

This game was created by Wolfgang Kramer, one of the most celebrated game designers in Germany, a country known for designing great games. Corsaro won the German Game of the Year award as the best children's game in 1991.

START

WELCOME TO SANTAIJANA

PIRATE ISLAND

SOLITAIRE

PLAYING

In this game, every move must capture a piece. You capture a piece by hopping over it. You can hop to the right, to the left, up, or down. You can't hop diagonally.

The piece you hop over has to be right next to the piece you are moving and you have to land on an empty circle. The piece you hop over is removed from the board.

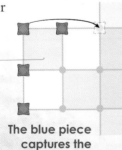

The blue piece captures the red piece by hopping over it.

You can move one piece, then switch to another piece for your next move — or not.

Keep hopping and removing pieces until there aren't any more moves to make. Remember: You can only move by hopping over other pieces.

WINNING

You win the game when there's only one playing piece left — and that piece is in the center of the board. But since this is a tough game to win, give yourself a pat on the back for progress toward that goal.

IF YOU HAVE...	YOU ARE...
One piece left in the center	A super-duper hopper
One piece left but it's not in the center	A super (but not duper) hopper
Two pieces left	A very hopeful hopper
Three pieces left	One hop short of hopeful
Four or more left	Ready to hop over to the hints to try a warm-up game

STUFF YOU DON'T NEED TO KNOW

Back in the late 1600s, the court of King Louis of France went nuts for this game. Today, it's played all over the world.

HINTS AND TIPS

Here are three warm-up games. Position the playing pieces as shown, then play as usual. Your goal is always to end up with only one piece in the center. You'll find solutions to these games and one way to win Solitaire on the inside back cover of this book.

Starting boards for warm-up games

MORE WAYS TO PLAY

Tired of trying to end up with only one piece? Change the rules and try to leave as many pieces as you can on the board. You can reach a dead end in just six moves, leaving 26 pieces on the board.

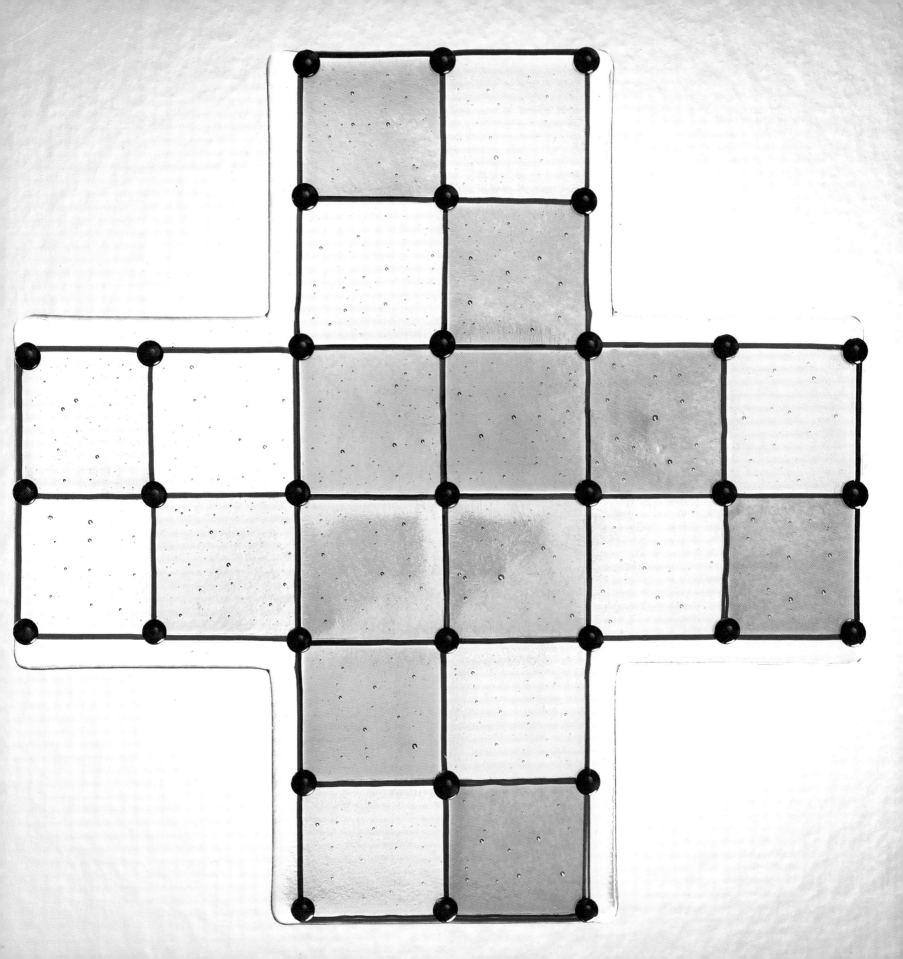

Two Ways to Play
PENTOMINOES

In 2006, 21 college students in Malaysia stuffed themselves into a MINI Cooper to set a new record. It's fun to cram a lot of stuff into a small space — which is what this game is about.

PENTOMINOES SOLITAIRE

PLAYERS 1

AGES 7 and up

PLAYING TIME 10–20 minutes

YOU NEED
All 12 pentominoes
(rhymes with dominoes)

PLAYING AND WINNING

Put all the pentominoes on the board with no overlaps and no pentominoes extending outside the board. Each pentomino must completely cover five squares on the board. You can place the pentomino in any position. You can even flip it over.

You **WIN** by fitting all the pentominoes on the board. Four squares will not be covered.

MORE WAYS TO PLAY SOLITAIRE

Arrange the pentominoes so that the board looks like each of these pictures. The white squares show the four squares that are not covered.

There are many solutions. Turn to pages 4 and 5 to see ours.

PENTOMINOES FOR TWO

PLAYERS 2

AGES 7 and up

PLAYING TIME 15 minutes

YOU NEED
All 12 pentominoes

SETUP
Spread the pentominoes out so you can see them all.

YOUR GOAL
Be the last to put a pentomino on the board.

PLAYING AND WINNING

Players take turns choosing a pentomino and placing it on the board. You can place the pentomino in any position. You can even flip it over.

Pentominoes can't overlap and can't extend outside the board. Each pentomino must completely cover five squares.

You **WIN** by placing a pentomino so that the other player can't find a spot to place another one. The last player to fit a pentomino on the board wins.

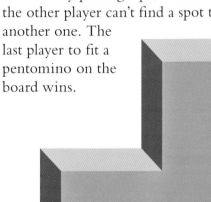

STUFF YOU DON'T NEED TO KNOW

Pente is the Greek word for five and *omino* is borrowed from the word "domino." These pentominoes are the only 12 shapes that can be made by joining five squares together at the edges. (If you don't believe us, try to come up with another one!)

HINTS AND TIPS

Solomon W. Golomb, the mathematician who invented the Pentominoes game, has this advice: If you don't know what to do, place a piece where it will make it even more difficult for your opponent to figure out what to do next.

TWO Morris GAMES

Three Men's Morris

Players 2

Ages 8 and up

Playing Time 10 minutes

You Need
3 playing pieces of one color

3 playing pieces of another color

Your Goal
Get three of your pieces in a row — horizontally, vertically, or diagonally.

Playing Three Men's Morris

At first, this game is like Tic-Tac-Toe. Players take turns putting a playing piece on a circle.

The first player cannot put a piece on the center circle (but the second player can).

When all three of your pieces are on the board, the game changes. On your turn, move one of your pieces along a line onto an empty circle. You can't move diagonally — only right, left, up, or down.

On your turn, you have to move — even if you don't like the moves that you can make.

Winning

To win, get three pieces in a row — horizontally, vertically, or diagonally.

Nine Men's Morris

Players 2

Ages 9 and up

Playing Time 20 minutes

You Need
9 playing pieces of one color

9 playing pieces of another color

Your Goal
Capture seven of your opponent's pieces

Playing Nine Men's Morris

In this game, you capture one of your opponent's pieces every time you get three in a row.

Players take turns putting a playing piece on a circle. When all nine pieces are on the board, the game changes. On your turn, move one of your pieces along any line onto an empty circle.

Capturing

A line of three pieces is called a **mill**. When you make a mill, you remove one of your opponent's pieces from the board.

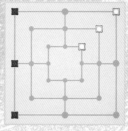

Red has made a mill — three in a row on a line. The white pieces aren't on a line, so they aren't a mill.

The piece you take can be anywhere on the board — except in a mill. Pieces that are in a mill can't be captured.

Flying

When a player has only three pieces left, those pieces gain a special power. Rather than just moving along a line to the next circle, those pieces can "**fly**" to any vacant circle on the board.

Winning

You win when the other player has only two pieces left. You can also win by blocking your opponent so no move is possible.

Hints and Tips

Once you form a mill, you can break it by moving one piece. On your next turn, move that piece back to form the mill again and make another capture. An even dirtier trick is the **double mill**, where breaking one mill lets you form a new mill.

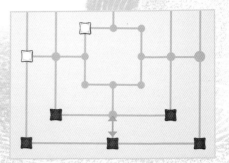

In this double mill, the middle red piece moves up on one turn and back down on the next, making a mill with each move.

Nine Men's Morris

Three Men's Morris

Stuff You Don't Need to Know
People all over the world play games like these. In Ghana, they play Achi; in the Philippines, it's called Tapatan; in Zimbabwe, they play Tsoro Yematatu, a three-in-a-row game that uses a triangular board.

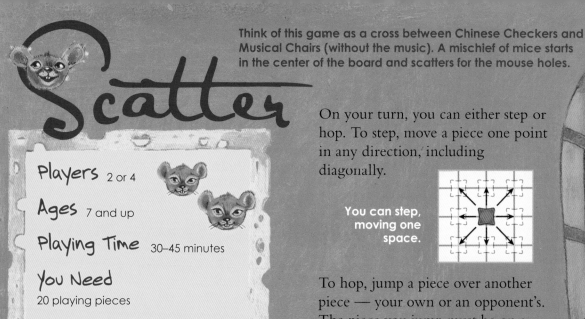

Scatter

Players 2 or 4

Ages 7 and up

Playing Time 30–45 minutes

You Need

20 playing pieces

2-player game: 10 pieces of the same color per player

4-player game: 5 pieces of the same color per player

Your Goal

Make sure that all your mice — that is, all your playing pieces — reach one of the green mouse holes at the edge of the board.

Playing

Choose a player to go first, then take turns placing pieces — one at a time — on the circles in the middle of the board.

After all 20 pieces are in place, the next player moves one of her pieces. Pieces move from point to point; a point is a place where the lines on the board cross.

On your turn, you can either step or hop. To step, move a piece one point in any direction, including diagonally.

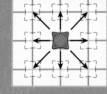

You can step, moving one space.

To hop, jump a piece over another piece — your own or an opponent's. The piece you jump must be on a point right next to you and you must land on an empty point. The jumped piece stays where it is — don't take it off the board.

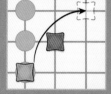

You can hop over a piece.

If you hop and land where you can make another hop in any direction, you can hop again. Or you can choose not to hop — it's up to you.

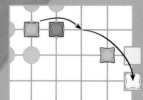

You can make multiple hops.

The line at the edge of the board is part of the playing area. You can move pieces onto points on this line.

Winning

To win, get all your mice to safety. There are 20 mice, 19 mouse holes, and room for one mouse in each hole. The player with the last piece on the board loses. (With four players, three players win!)

Hints and Tips

Set up a line of pieces that lets a series of hops carry you to safety. But watch out! Your opponent could use that same series of hops to beat you to a mouse hole.

Stuff You Don't Need to Know

When this game was invented in the 18th century, it was called Conspirators. The original board showed a room with doors. To escape, each piece needed to sneak away through a door.

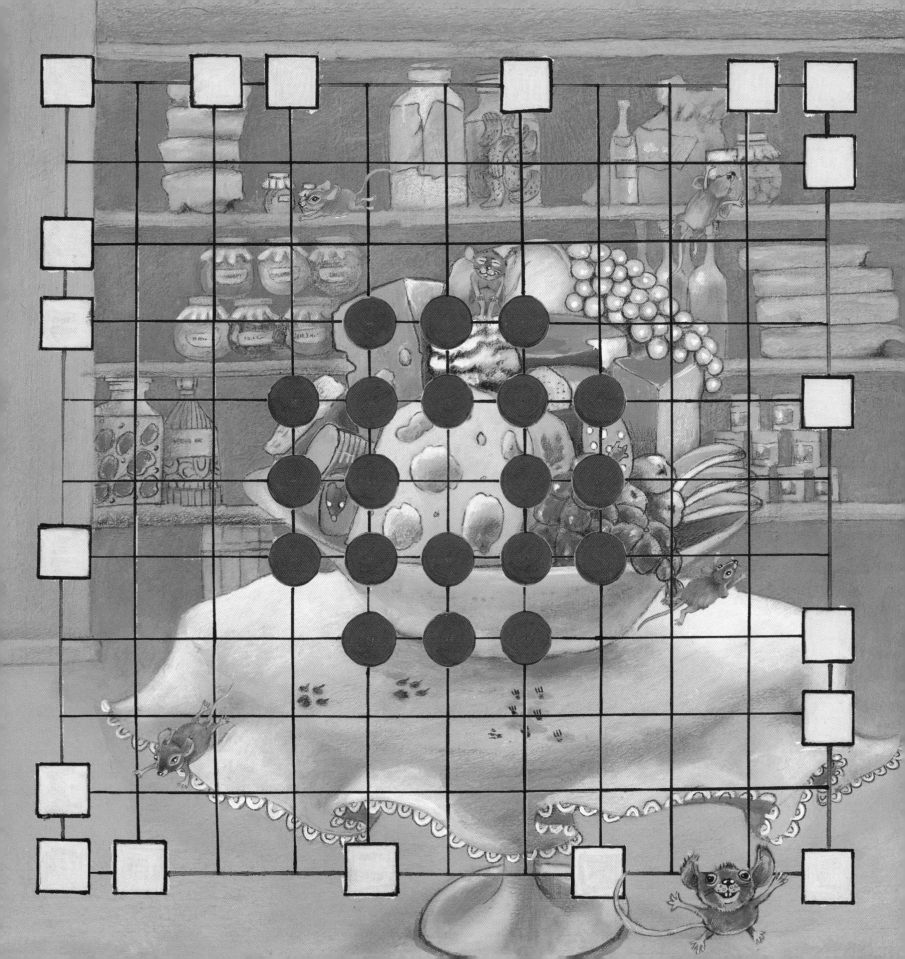

Tigers & Goats

*In Nepal, this game is called **baagchaal**.*
***Baag** means "tiger" and **chaal** means "movement."*

Players 2

Ages 8 and up

Playing Time 10–20 minutes

You Need
4 pieces of one color (tigers)
20 pieces of another color (goats)

Setup
Put the four tigers on the spaces at the corners of the board.

Your Goal
Goats want to surround tigers.
Tigers want to eat goats.

Playing

First, decide who will be the tigers and who will be the goats.

Next, agree on how many goats the tigers must eat to win. Stubborn goats may not give up until the tigers eat 11 of the 20 goats — when only nine goats remain, the goats can't surround the tigers and win. Goats that are in a hurry can admit defeat after five of the 20 goats are eaten.

The player with the goats goes first by placing a goat on any empty space.

Then it's the tigers' turn. A tiger can move in two ways: It can move along any line to the next empty space or it can eat a goat by jumping over it.

The jumping tiger must start from right beside a goat, must jump in a straight line, and must land on the empty space on the goat's other side. The jump must follow the lines on the board. If there isn't a line, the tiger **can't** make that jump. When a tiger jumps a goat, the goat is taken off the board.

Whenever a tiger moves into a position to jump a goat, the tiger has to warn the goat by **roaring**!

Once all the goats are on the board, a goat can move along any line to the next empty space.

A Few More Rules

If a tiger can eat a goat, the tiger must eat the goat. A tiger can only eat one goat in a turn. A tiger can't jump over a tiger. Goats can't jump.

Winning

The goats win by surrounding the tigers so they can't move. The tigers win by eating the agreed upon number of goats. The game is a tie if none of the goats can move or if either player moves a piece between the same two spaces more than five times in a row.

In this game, the goats (red) have won. The tigers (blue) can't move.

Hints and Tips

In your first few games, you may think the tigers have an advantage. After another game or two, you may change your mind.

Wise tigers spread out.
Smart goats stick together.

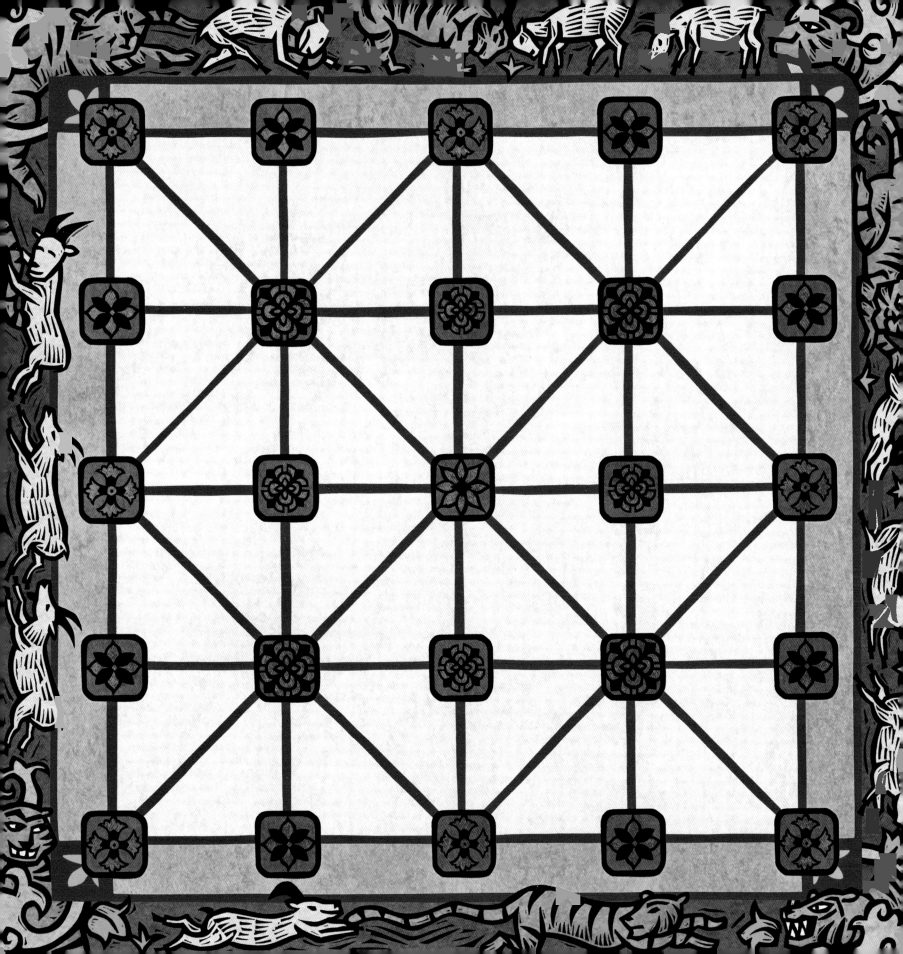

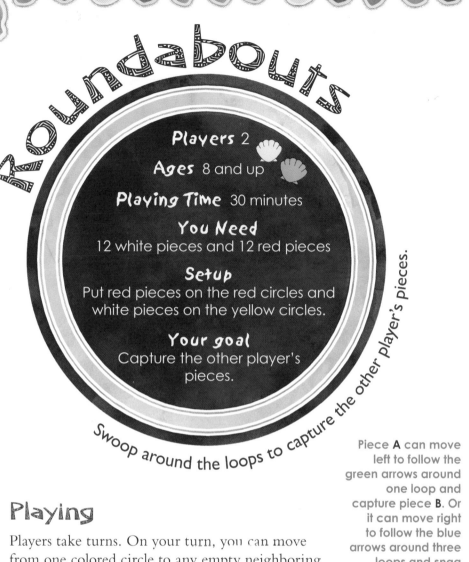

Roundabouts

Players 2

Ages 8 and up

Playing Time 30 minutes

You Need
12 white pieces and 12 red pieces

Setup
Put red pieces on the red circles and white pieces on the yellow circles.

Your goal
Capture the other player's pieces.

Swoop around the loops to capture the other player's pieces.

Playing

Players take turns. On your turn, you can move from one colored circle to any empty neighboring circle or you can swoop around a loop to capture one of your opponent's pieces.

You can move a piece one space in any direction, including diagonally.

To capture a piece, your piece **must** travel around a loop and land on your opponent's piece. Your piece must start on the loop it will travel around.

You can travel around a loop **only** if you are going to make a capture.

You can travel around as many loops as you like — as long as no pieces are in the way. When you capture a piece, take it off the board.

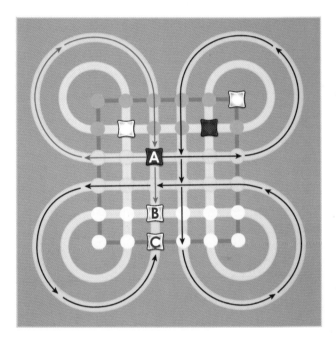

Piece **A** can move left to follow the green arrows around one loop and capture piece **B**. Or it can move right to follow the blue arrows around three loops and snag piece **C**.

Winning

You win by capturing all the other player's pieces. The winner's score is equal to the pieces he or she has left on the board. The loser's score is zero.

We suggest you play a match, which is two games. Alternate who moves first and combine your scores for both games. The highest combined score wins the match.

FANORONA

This game starts out fast and furious with many casualties on both sides. Then it settles down to a slower, more thoughtful game.

Players **2**

Ages **9** and up

Playing Time **30** minutes

You Need

22 white pieces
22 red pieces

Setup

Put the red pieces on the black dots and the white pieces on the beige dots.

Your Goal

Capture your opponent's pieces.

Playing

Players take turns. On your turn, move one of your pieces along a line onto the next dot. (The space has to be empty for your piece to move onto it.)

You can capture your opponent's pieces by approaching them or by moving away from them. When you capture a piece, take it off the board.

Capture by Approaching

Move your piece toward your opponent's piece so that it ends up right next to the piece. You'll capture that piece — and all the pieces stretching in an unbroken line away from it along the line of your movement.

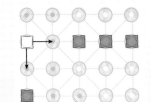

This white piece can move right and capture three red pieces. Or it can move down and capture one.

Capture by Retreating

Starting from beside your opponent's piece, move your piece away from it. You'll capture the piece that was next to your piece — and all the pieces stretching in an unbroken line away from it along the line of your movement.

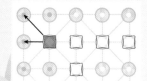

This red piece can move left and capture three white pieces. Or it can move on the diagonal and capture one.

Take Your Pick

If you make a move that gives you both a retreating capture and an approaching capture, you must choose which one to take. You can't take both.

Making Multiple Captures

On your very first move, your turn ends after your first capture. But on all other turns, you can make several captures as long as you move the same piece each time, the piece changes direction with each move, and you don't move the piece back to any of the dots it was on earlier.

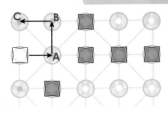

This white piece moves to dot A and captures three red pieces by approaching. Then, it moves to dot B, capturing one piece by retreating. Finally, it moves to dot C to capture another piece by retreating.

Winning

You win by capturing all of your opponent's pieces.

Special Rule to Avoid a Tie

You can't move a piece back and forth between two dots on consecutive turns. If you move from dot A to dot B on one turn, you can't move back to dot A on your next turn.

Leveling the Field

Let the weaker player go first — and give that player one extra move at the beginning of the game

Stuff You Don't Need to Know

This is the national game of Madagascar, an island off the coast of Africa. According to legend, a dying king called his two sons to his bedside. Whichever son arrived first would inherit the throne. The older son was playing Fanorona and didn't want to leave the game — so he lost the kingdom.

China Moon

Like frogs in a pond, your pieces hop from lily pad to lily pad.

Players 2 to 5

Ages 8 and up

Playing Time 30–45 minutes

You Need

3 playing pieces of the same color for each player

14 water lily tokens (4 yellow, 4 pink, 4 white, 1 black, 1 blue)

Setup

Place a yellow lily, a pink lily, and a white lily on numbers 1, 2, and 3 in the big lily pad in the center of the board. It doesn't matter which color goes on which number. Put the blue lily on number 4.

Put the black lily on the lily pad marked with the black lily. Place the other lily tokens at random on the lily pads that are marked with lilies.

Players place their pieces at the start.

Your Goal

Gather the bouquet of lilies that earns the most points. You want the lucky blue lily and as many matching lilies as you can. You don't want the black lily — it's worth negative points.

Hints and Tips

Look for moves that let you make many captures with the same piece.

30

Playing

Players take turns. When it's your turn, you move three different playing pieces. You always have to move one piece that belongs to another player. The other two pieces can be your own or someone else's — it's up to you. You move each piece forward two steps.

Only one playing piece can be on each lily pad. As you move a piece along the track, hop it over any pieces that are in the way and land in the next space without a piece.

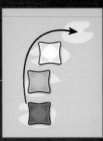

This move counts as one step even though red hopped over two lily pads.

You only move forward, never backward.

Follow the instructions in the chart to the right when you land on a lily token, frog, cricket, or butterfly.

Special Spaces

If your piece lands on a...	You have to do this...
Lily token	Take the lily. If the token was on top of a frog, cricket, or butterfly, then follow the instructions for that animal, too.
Frog	Trade a lily with another player for a lily of a different color. You choose which lily to give away and which lily to take, but you have to trade — even if you don't want to. If you have no lilies or if no other players have lilies, don't do anything.
Cricket	Move two more steps forward.
Butterfly	Leave a lily of your choice on the first lily pad before the butterfly space that isn't occupied by a playing piece. If you have no lilies, don't do anything.

You have to follow these instructions even if you weren't the one who moved your piece onto the space.

Ending the Game

The owner of the first piece to arrive at the big lily pad in the center collects the lily from number 1. The second piece collects the lily from number 2, the third from number 3, and the fourth piece collects the blue lily.

You don't have to land on the big lily pad on an exact count.

Winning

When the fourth piece reaches the center, the game ends — even if there are still water lilies and playing pieces on the board. Whoever has the most points wins the game. Here's how to calculate your points:

Blue water lily = 4 points
One yellow, pink, or white lily= 1 point
Two matching lilies = 3 points
Three matching lilies = 6 points
Four matching lilies = 10 points
Black lily = negative 2 points

Hints and Tips

You can trade or leave behind the black lily (which is worth negative points) just like any other water lily.

Think about how moving other players' pieces can help you out. Think about how hopping can help you move forward faster.

Stuff You Don't Need to Know

The inventor of China Moon, a Frenchman named Bruno Faidutti, is also known as the Professor of Chaos. When you play China Moon, don't be surprised if there are sudden upsets — the person who seems to be winning can quickly lose her advantage and the person who's behind can suddenly shoot ahead.

Embrace the chaos. It's part of the fun.

1 Everyday Checkers

Your Goal

Capture all of your opponent's checkers.

Playing

Players take turns. Each time it's your turn, you can move or jump and capture. Ordinary checkers ALWAYS move or jump toward the opposite side of the board. Checkers always stay on the blue squares.

Move a checker diagonally one square, always toward your opponent's side of the board. ▶

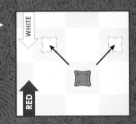

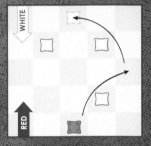

◀ *Capture your opponent's checkers by jumping over them. Checkers always jump diagonally toward your opponent's side of the board. Keep jumping until you can't jump again.*

Take captured checkers off the board.

If you can capture one of your opponent's checkers, you MUST make the jump. If there's a choice, you decide which capture to make.

When a checker reaches the last row on your opponent's side of the board, it becomes a king. Crown it with an extra piece of the same color.

A king moves and jumps like an ordinary checker — except a king can move or

Stack two pieces to make a king.

jump toward either side of the board and can change direction between jumps. Like any other checker, a king can be jumped and captured.

Winning

You win by capturing all of your opponent's checkers or blocking them so they can't move.

2 Givaway Checkers

Your Goal

Lose all of your checkers.

Playing

Except for the goal of the game, Giveaway Checkers is played just like Everyday Checkers.

Winning

In this game, the winner is the biggest loser. To win, make your opponent capture all of your checkers.

3 Super King Checkers

Your Goal

Capture all of your opponent's checkers.

Playing

Players take turns moving their checkers just as they did in Everyday Checkers.

Make captures by jumping as you do in Everyday Checkers. But in Super King Checkers, ordinary checkers can jump away from the opposite side of the board as well as toward it. A checker can make multiple captures in any combination of backward and forward jumps. If you can make a capture, you **must** make it.

If a checker ends its move on the last row of the board on the opposite side, that piece becomes a Super King. Crown it with an extra piece of the same color.

The Super King's Super Powers

A Super King can move any distance along a diagonal line in any direction. If one of your opponent's checkers is in the way, the Super King can jump and capture it and keep on moving. As long as the Super King stays on the same diagonal, it can travel over any number of empty squares on either side of a jump.

A Super King can make multiple jumps. If a second jump is available, the Super King can change direction and move on a new diagonal to make that jump.

But there are limits to super powers. (Even Superman is vulnerable to kryptonite.) After a jump, a Super King can change direction and move on a new diagonal **only if** a jump is available on that diagonal.

There are two more ways to stop a rampaging Super King. A Super King can only jump the opponent's pieces. And even a Super King can't jump two enemy checkers at the same time.

When a Super King jumps more than one checker, the checkers that are jumped stay on the board until the end of the turn. This is important since a Super King can't jump the same checker twice.

In a single turn, this red Super King can jump three of the white checkers, but not the fourth.

This red Super King can't move in any direction. A red checker blocks one direction and a pair of white checkers blocks the other.

Winning

You win by capturing all of your opponent's checkers or blocking them so they can't move.

Start

Finish

1 2 3 4

CHECKERS

There are dozens of ways to play Checkers. Here are our favorites. You may know the first one, but you probably don't know the other two.

For All Three Versions

Players 2

Ages 8 and up

Playing Time 30 minutes

You Need

12 red playing pieces
12 white playing pieces
A few extra pieces of each color

Setup

Place the pieces on the 12 blue squares in the first three rows on opposites sides of the board — red on one side, white on the other

Stuff You Don't Need to Know

People all over the world have created different ways to play Checkers, including Russian Checkers, Turkish Checkers, Spanish Checkers, and Armenian Checkers. Invent your own set of rules and you could become the proud inventor of (Insert Your Name Here) Checkers.

Push Penny Bounce

Try your penny-pushing skills in this pint-sized version of a game that King Henry VIII of England used to play.

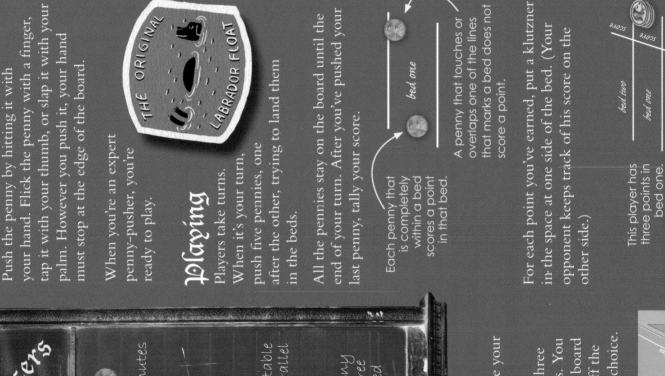

Penny Bouncers

NEXT UP

Players 2
Ages 8 and up
Playing Time 15 minutes

You Need
a table
5 pennies
18 klutzners

Setup
Lay the book flat on the table with the starting line parallel to the table's edge.

Your Goal
Be the first to land a penny three times (and only three times) in each bed marked on the board.

Practice

Before you start playing, practice your penny pushing.

Look at the board and find the three beds, the areas separated by lines. You want to slide a penny across the board into a bed. You can bounce it off the book's wire coil or not — your choice.

Place a penny flat on the board like this.

Push the penny by hitting it with your hand. Flick the penny with a finger, tap it with your thumb, or slap it with your palm. However you push it, your hand must stop at the edge of the board.

When you're an expert penny-pusher, you're ready to play.

Playing
Players take turns. When it's your turn, push five pennies, one after the other, trying to land them in the beds.

All the pennies stay on the board until the end of your turn. After you've pushed your last penny, tally your score.

Each penny that is completely within a bed scores a point in that bed.

A penny that touches or overlaps one of the lines that marks a bed does not score a point.

For each point you've earned, put a klutzner in the space at one side of the bed. (Your opponent keeps track of his score on the other side.)

This player has three points in bed one.

If a penny doesn't reach the first line on the board, that play doesn't count. Try again.

If you push a penny off the board, too bad. You don't get to do that one over.

Your goal is to get three points in each bed. Once you have three points, each additional penny in that bed scores a point for your opponent. If your opponent already has three points in the bed, no one scores. There's an exception to this: If that extra point would give your opponent the winning point, it doesn't count for anyone.

Winning
You win by being the first player to score three points in each of the three beds.

Leveling the Field
If one player usually wins, give the underdog a better chance by letting him have a few do-overs: If he doesn't like where a penny lands, he can flick that penny again. Before you start playing, agree on how many do-overs the underdog gets.

Stuff You Don't Need to Know
King Henry VIII played Shovelboard, a game in which players shoved metal weights down tables that were up to 30 feet long.

starting line

bed one
score

bed two
score

bed three
score

Credits

Tiger wrangler	Pat Murphy
Goat herder	Corie Thompson
Art drover	Kate Paddock
Super checker	Jen Mills
Zookeeper	Kelly Shaffer
Master of the 2nd dimension	Sara Boore
Master of the 3rd dimension	David Avidor
Photography	Peter Fox
Ever-so-able assistant	Laurie Bryan
Ever-so-able intern	Kate Phillips
Keeper of the turkey crossing	John Cassidy
Game gurus	R. Wayne Schmittberger and Mark Jackson
Permissions	Marybeth Arago
Inspiration	Sid Sackson, who helped choose the games for the first edition of this book
Cover design	Michael Sherman

Illustration & Photo Credits

Hoppers	Adam Gustavson
Game of Y	Photo ©Charles Hewitt/ Hulton Archive/Getty Images
The Royal Game of Ur	Ande Cook
Surround	Dave Garbot
Corsaro	Robin Ator; parchment and quill photo ©Martin Fox/Index Stock
Solitaire	Janet Hiebert
Pentominoes	José Cruz
Morris	Raul Colón
Scatter	Elena Schern
Tigers & Goats	Sue Todd
Roundabouts	Steve Kongsle
Fanorona	Gregg Valley
China Moon	Miriam Elze
Checkers	Ian Phillips
Push Penny Bounce	Coaster art: Marc Rosenthal; Dog models: Billy "The Bulldog" Melton, Martini Chorba, and Maxwell B. Thompson; chalkboard ©SassyStock Photos/Fotosearch

Game Credits

Hoppers (also known as Halma) by Dr. George Howard Monks; Mini Hoppers by M. Winther

Game of Y by Craige Schensted and Charles Titus. A more challenging game board for Game of Y is available from Kadon Enterprises at www.gamepuzzles.com. Our game board is used with permission from Mudcrack Y & Poly-Y, published by NEO Press.

Surround by R. Wayne Schmittberger

Corsaro by Wolfgang Kramer

Pentominoes and the Pentomino game were invented by Dr. Solomon W. Golomb and are used here with permission

Scatter board designed by R. Wayne Schmittberger

China Moon by Bruno Faidutti

Special Thanks

Many thanks to all who play-tested games, especially the game testers at El Carmelo Elementary School, the game-happy Klutzniks, the always playful Exploratorium staffers, and the many friends and family members who played with us. And thanks to all who offered advice, including Aaron Lawn of End Game and the friendly gamers on BoardGameGeek (www.boardgamegeek.com). Thanks to Natalie Hill, Carole Lawson and Kayt de Fever.

Models

Flora Cabili	Matt O'Reilly
Marcel Colchen	Larry Richardson, Jr.
Herb Kaiser	Debbi Sizemore
Jerusha Krebs	Robert Smith
Brianna Lee	Michael Starr
Leslyn S. Leong	Jill Turney
Arne Lim	Annie Vesey